FEEDBACK

Food for champions
Four practical methods

Frans Knoben

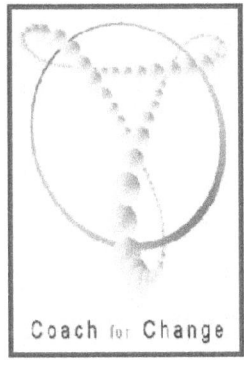

Colophon

© Frans Knoben

Summer 2010

ISBN 978-1-4457-6907-3

www.coachforchange.nl

info@coachforchange.nl

Printing house: LuLu

MEANT IS STILL NOT BEEN SAID

SAID IS STILL NOT BEEN HEARD

HEARD IS STILL NOT BEEN UNDERSTOOD

UNDERSTOOD IS STILL NOT AGREED

AGREED IS STILL NOT BEEN DONE

Feedback, food for champions

FOREWORD by Harry Dirks

Feedback is the process by which any organism rules itself towards its aim or destiny. A process of integration of the different parts of this organism, system or organization. This counts for plants and animals, as well as for individual human beings and for groups of humans like teams. The feedback in plants and animals is in-born or build-in. And since human-beings have their roots in the animal structure, we consider that humans have also an inborn feedback.

We human beings however are also able to reflect and to be conscious. As a result of this reflection and consciousness we discover what we call 'free will' and response-ability.
We are able to make our choices…
The question here is how our inborn and unconscious feedback holds and maintains together with this 'free will' and response-ability. As we see the results of our choices, it certainly is not clear and obvious if our ability to reflect and to be respons-able works out as a gain or a loss for humans and for mankind.
Our choices and 'respons-ability' do not seem to rule us towards our aim and destiny, as build-in feedback does. Instead of saving ourselves and saving our souls (S.O.S.) these so called 'free will'-decisions bring us much conflict and (self)destruction. It looks like that we have lost our feedback.

Frans Knoben has seen, heard and understood this and he shows , how to restore our feedback-ability. Feedback is an intrapersonal as well as an interpersonal process. In both positions the key of the restauration of our feedback is the development of our ability to Listen. (Listen and obey to the signals that feed our build-in feedback process)

Frans emphasizes "listen" consciously to yourself, the others around you and your situation and get in touch with your inborn feedback processes to creatively find out about what and how to reach your targets and goals and the fulfillment of your tasks, mission and destiny.

He has a superb track doing this. And I wish him and his readers/students lots of success.

Harry – Hardeep Singh – Dirks,
Clinical Psychologist and Gestalt Psychotherapist; Teacher Kundalini-Yoga.

Feeding back on Feedback
L. Michael Hall, Ph.D.

You know it and I know it— *giving feedback* is not easy and *receiving feedback* is a hundred times harder yet. That's not a revelation. And saying it really does not help any of us. So what does?

What enables you and I to provide high quality feedback is a new informed understanding of its value, what it really is, and having some practical processes whereby we can receive and provide it in a way that makes it an accelerator of development and self-actualization. And that's what Frans Knoben has provided in *Feedback: Food For Champions* (2010).

I am delighted to recommend this small practical book which provides as simple a way as possible to the subject of feedback. I'm also delighted to see his use of *The Axes of Change Model* in this book and to relate it to this essential skill. Originally I designed the *Axes of Change* model after modeling how some expert coaches for their ability to facilitate generative change with their clients. Based on four meta-programs of NLP, the model enables a person to know and effectively work with the four change mechanisms for psychologically healthy people— motivation, decision, creation, and integration. Here Frans has applied the model for learning a new way of responding to feedback. Very creative!

What will you find in this book? You will find a list of specific things to provide top-notch feedback and you will also find a list for how to screw up feedback. I liked that second one! Making that list explicit really blows the whistle on those behaviors that mess things up and so, the behaviors to eliminate if you want to become excellence in this expertise.

In this work, Frans has emphasized how to communicate with precision— in sensory-based terms, how to take responsibility, how to use "I" language, how to create a safe context, and many, many other specific qualities that make for high quality feedback. You'll also find here that the processes for receiving and giving feedback are the very processes for effectively handling conflict and creating more intimacy in relationships.

Something that you will probably find surprising and delightful is the discussion of *appreciative feedback*. This is missing in most discussions about feedback and so provides an excellent and needed balance. Feedback isn't only for problems and confrontations. It's for building relationships and human capital. It's an expression of emotional intelligence.

Because we emphasize in Meta-Coach Training receiving and giving feedback as two of the core seven coaching skills, in every country that I've taken Meta-Coaching, the question of the "feedback sandwich" comes up. Frans also deals with that here and warns, as I do, against using it! Surprising? The fact is that the "feedback sandwich" is not a clean way to give feedback. If that surprises you, you'll be sure to want to read that discussion.

Finally, I was interested in reading Frans' use of *The Axes of Change Model* in the context of learning, especially about learning a new way to do something (which is what generative "change" is all about). That was not the original design of the Model, so it is fascinating to see it utilized for that purpose. And Frans' descriptions perfectly fits with the design of the Model.

Here's to your developing excellence in this critical skill for relationships and conflict resolution— may you become increasingly competent in receiving and giving feedback.

L. Michael Hall, Ph.D.
(ISNS) International Society of Neuro-Semantics
The International Meta-Coach System
www.self-actualizing.org

PREFACE

Giving and receiving feedback, a whole bookshelf can be filled with books explaining theories, techniques and backgrounds. Google on the Internet and you'll find all the information you need.

But despite all this knowledge you can still ask the question: "Why is giving or receiving feedback so difficult?"

> *"feedback, the food for champions"*

Without feedback there'll be no great performances or development. Feedback has a major role in all contexts where people cooperate: In business, at home, in sports, in healthcare, at school, in public services, in all situations where relationships occur. And you just have to look at your work, in your relationships or with your children to see it happen. But providing feedback seems to be very difficult. Emotions play a role and because you don't know how the other will respond to your feedback, this will often create withdraw behavior. Even with all the knowledge we have, despite all those books, it still appears to be a difficult job. Apparently, knowledge alone is not enough. Besides knowing how to give feedback, there should be a way to learn this competence. We have methods and exercises enough, but about the whole process of learning these skills and competences there is little to be found.

One learning method is described in this book : the "axes of change" model. This method provides surprisingly good results. This generative change process includes steps of motivation, decision-making, creation and solidification.

The 'axes of change model' is a very helpful approach in the learning of competences and it gives great insight into the underlying learning steps. In practice it will turn out that exercising over and over again (as the mother of all learning) is needed. In the beginning, you'll then reluctantly give feedback, but soon you notice that the skill improves, until it suddenly appears to be present at an unconscious level in your behavior.

In this book the focus is on applying the skills of giving and receiving feedback. It provides four great feedback techniques in a compact form. Briefly and concisely written, with a step-by-step approach. And also a whole set of tips, insights, advices, attitudes and mindsets that are very suitable in feedback situations. No great theories, only directly usable stuff! Use it, enjoy applying, learn and learn with regular 'party-time' and become a champion feedbacker!

Frans Knoben
founder & trainer CoachforChange
summer 2010

> *Two eyes and two ears to observe.*
> *One mouth to judge!*
> CONFUCIUS

Thank you

I would like to thank many people.

But the most important are:

o   My partner Loes, for all, I love you;

o   Ingrid Ronken, my dear niece for all her help in editing and translating, thank you, thank you;

o   L. Michael Hall, for all your innovative ideas;

o   Nisandeh Neta, who triggered me to "close the knowing- doing gap";

o   Harry Dirks, for all your advices, satanama!

Thank you all!

Frans Knoben

1

COMMUNICATION SKILLS

1.1 Listening & feedback

- *Two ears to listen, just one mouth to speak.*
- *For a bad listener half a word is enough.*
- *Speaking is silver, (listening) silence is gold.*

Listening is one of the key skills in communication. Listening is a condition for giving feedback. Without listening there's no feedback.

The garden of feedback

Giving feedback is just like gardening. Compare a team with a garden. Many times we assemble a whole lot of plants, trees and bushes. In the beginning all of them grow and try to get a good place. In the sun, enough water, growing and minimizing others. The gardener sees all these things happen and receives the feedback through the result of this wild, unleaded, not supported growth in his domain. He knows that the roots should always be placed at the best possible place; the tree trunk should have just a few, major branches. Taking care of a place with enough or maybe less sun will stimulate the growth of the plant. And when this all happens the result will be fruits, flowers, marvelous to be seen, in a perfect match besides and behind each other. But when a branch wants too much space, it will be pruned back again. During the years there will always be the process of pruning, replacing, supporting and leading. The best gardeners do it all the time, not once a month. Every day looking around and seeing what happens in the garden. Seeing what went well, seeing what might go wrong. The way the gardener looks around in his garden is the same as listening and looking around in a team. Cutting branches, leading (or coaching) other branches, giving extra support where necessary, giving specific nutrients. One plant nitrogen, the other calcium, et cetera. Not too much, not too less. Every plant in its own pace, in its own season.

Just like the gardener, the manager is the one who should listen very well to his employees. Give them what they need to grow and to flourish, each individual in its own pace and at the right time. Sometimes you have to stop one, other times you lead, coach or support one.

In giving and receiving feedback you really have to apply the listening skill. When you don't, you're probably just busy with your own position and intentions will be lost. The other isn't heard and understood well and miscommunication is the result. Without listening you won't establish a real contact and information will be lost. The result is that cooperation suffers and relationships are stiff.

If you don't listen when feedback is given to you, you won't understand the intention of what is said, or what is tried to signal non-verbally. There's no dialogue taking place, just a one-way-communication. Without listening, a reply can't be seen as feedback, but probably you'll give unsolicited advices.

The listening skill is a difficult one. You really need to do something. For example someone is talking to you and while you're listening, you're not supposed to ask examination questions, which will interrupt his story. This seems to be a real challenge for many people. People tend to ask, to reply, to interact and then of course, the listening stops. Or, what happens more often, the thinking process reacts on the spoken words. The next step is creating a thought stream in the mind and at the same time distracting attention from the conversation; especially in case of discussions or conflicting thoughts between people. This causes a lack of discipline to really listen in a non-defensive way. Just leave home the ego. Listening to what is actually said, instead of what you think that has been said. At the same time judgments appear, which are often based on a lack or shortage of information or due to former (equal) situations. Listening in a non-judging way is obviously a less developed skill for many people. That means that there's still a lot of work to do and a lot to learn for many of us.

Besides this ability to listen accurately, not to be defensive or judgmental, you should listen carefully by:

- focusing your attention outward to others. Also listen with your eyes, through eye contact and to zoom in on any non-verbal expression of the other person;
- giving yourself reasons why it's important to listen well. You should do it in such a way that you create interest and involvement. This will facilitate applying the listening skill.
- stopping the own thinking process when the other speaks. Thinking distracts, the attention isn't in the relation anymore, but in your own mind. The reason why this often happens is just the idea that you should have thought about what you'll have to respond. This is only partly true.

The brain of the human being is a wonderful thing. We can talk about 100 to 150 words per minute and the limitations are only caused by the facial muscles (and fortunately too). However, within one minute we're able to process between 1000 to 10,000 possible words and phrases in the mind by mind movies. All those movies in the mind[1] process the information much faster than the spoken word. There's always enough time to consult your mind while you're speaking. Definitely when you start your reply in your mind you can build your story while speaking. The effect is that you'll be able to pay full attention to the other and listen continuously and accurately.

- learning to listen to two things:

  the content   → what someone actually says, what is the message

  the structure   →structure, how someone says something,

              the form, the packaging.

- listening to what is not said, what is omitted, but still meant. Listening between the lines means pure listening as well as listening to the heart (what about the other person, what do you think he is feeling?). But check these assumptions too, because otherwise you pretend to be a mind reader.

- 'listening' with all your senses. See, hear, feel, smell and notice.

- 'listening' to all those non-verbal signals the other shows. Breathing (chest-belly, fast-slow), pitch, volume, the body movement, the brightness and so on.

- listening followed by talking including silence-breaks. Breaks are needed

---

[1] L. Michael Hall Ph.D., Movie Mind: directing the theater of your mind, 2002

to organize thoughts; for both yourself and others. Give others the chance and the opportunity to think, reflect, or to notice how his feelings and emotions play a role.

- using your voice while listening, so the other knows that you're still there and involved. Use humming, yes, yes, yes, OK, yep, etc. as supporting expressions. Just like nodding your head, without suggesting that you agree with what is told. Show in your posture that you are and stay fully committed and focused to his story.

- listening with an observational, non judgmental attitude. So you can observe and record everything unfiltered.

- summarizing and checking whether you've understood the other well and by asking questions all the way.

- asking questions for clarification, not for discussion. Ask questions and again questions. The listener has a great partner in the questioner. And make sure you listen carefully to the answers. Asking questions is designed to get the complete picture and to allow the other to tell you what he thinks is necessary to be understood. Use the open style questions, what, where, who, when, how, which. It gives the floor to the speaker and you'll receive all the information you want.

1.2 Observing or judging

From childhood on we learn to judge. In raising their kids the parents start the right and wrong game already in the early years. You're not allowed to do this or that otherwise you will get punished. And also giving rewards is related to the good & bad issue. You receive a hug or sweets as a reward for something you have done well. In the day-care centre and at school this continues at a great pace. The measuring rod of good and wrong is clearly present in that period.

Maybe you've had a lot of punishment at school or you've seen other children being punished. Or were you the child that perfectly obeyed to the rules of right and wrong? Being judged of being right or wrong is the common way we all grew up. And then there's the moment we discover that we can judge very quickly. Entire courses and skills are based on thinking quickly (think of all those time limited examinations at school) and making quick judgments is an obviously desired skill. Until we learn that there are areas where quick thinking, quick deciding isn't the right thing to do. In interacting with people, in disagreements, arguments or in feedback you'll discover that judging has many disadvantages. Just try to consider this. Presumably you'll find that in all those heated, angry, stressed and exited conversations there's always the same problem. You have an opinion about something or about what is said by another person and vice versa. Something is done wrong, something is said wrong or there was the use of offending words (at least he experienced the words in that way), or there's an insight you don't agree with or somebody looked angry and you think they don't understand a thing about that situation. Always judging. And judging itself is OK. The internal part, as a result of the process of all you learned and experienced in the past, will undoubtedly lead to judgments. And because you can't ignore the past, it's always there. But the external judging is the problem causer.

You are...; what you do is......; you can't .....; you have to ......, all comments to what the other should do, should change and only based on judgments. In his books about constructive language in relationships,

Thomas Gordon refers to this as the 'you-messages', which create problems in relations.

Instead of just responding to what we see or hear our first reaction is almost always a judgmental one. Neutral and clean perception fades into the background. In this way we unintentionally cause many unnecessary conflicts and stressful situations. Working together, living together is only possible when we talk about the things we encounter. Luckily this often happens, but frequently we also need to give each other feedback. And then it appears that giving snap judgments is an unpleasant habit and a persistent one. Even when you decide you really want to get rid of it, even when you say that to yourself a thousand times a day, you seem to be stuck with it. The moment you discover this habit, you know you have to correct your communication style. You have to learn again how to perceive things open-mindedly. If this happens at an early age you really are a lucky one. Because then, in all phases of your future life, you'll have a lot of benefits of it. In all your life roles: the employee, the boss, the father, the mother, the husband, wife or partner, the friend and so on.

Learning to make a real assessment is possible by focusing on only the things you perceive purely with all your senses. So just tell yourself what you see, hear, feel, smell, taste and note. Name this without being judgmental and question yourself "what should I infer? What do you mean?"

- Judgments based on too little information are the same as expressions of prejudice.
- Postponement of judgment should be the attitude.
- Checking of what you think you perceived is what has to be done.
- Any judgment before the last or final judgment is prejudice.

1.3 Kindness & Curiosity

What we really need in order to understand each other better is curiosity. With genuine curiosity we can discover new things in the other. And this discovery will many times turn out to be enjoyable, challenging and sometimes confrontational because a new world will be opened for you. You'll learn to understand one another (and yourself) much better. You show that you're truly interested in him or her. By being really curious you'll get more information from and about the other. The other one wants to start a dialogue with you and provides you more information as well. Many times this information influences you immediately and sometimes a discovery of how you respond and interact is initiated.

When curiosity is combined with a kind attitude, the doors open. Nobody can resist genuine friendliness. Consider the expression: *"kindness is difficult to give away, for it is usually returned* [2]*."*

Do a test and treat people with genuine kindness for a while. Note what happens and how people find this surprisingly pleasant and how they respond in a similar way.

---

[2] Mark Ortman

1.4 Congruency

The way you speak determines how a message will be understood. An angry tone or a friendly tone makes all the difference. Non-verbally, we're able to support everything we say, strengthening or weakening.

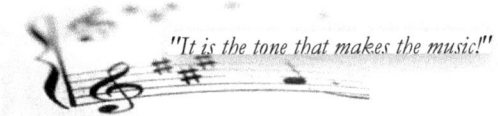

"It is the tone that makes the music!"

The attitude, the movements, the sounds, the gestures and eye-expressions largely determine the significance of what you say. If someone is congruent in its non-verbal and verbal communication then this strengthens the effect. You see, hear and notice that it is real. There are no hidden meanings or suspicious behavior. When someone says something that he actually does not agree with, then you'll see that in his body language. We'll notice this incongruent behavior and you conclude that there's something wrong. This means that, also in giving feedback, besides words the whole body contributes. Professional actors may still try to represent things differently. They are trained to play a certain role. But we, the ordinary people in ordinary everyday situations, we are rarely aware of such a role-play and we just do our thing. This means that the non-verbal communication as an interpreter of how we feel is very visible and audible. If we say A while we think and feel B, B will be visible or audible in non-verbal signs. You see something strange, there's incongruence in the behavior, leading to doubt about the sincerity of what is said.

The opposite is also true. Sometimes you see passionate speakers telling their story. The body, the gestures, the enthusiasm, the inspiration is clearly visible in the movements. The tone is lively and fascinating, and so on, thus creating full congruency in the communication.

1.5 Non-verbal support

The facial expressions cause many people to be an open book related to their thinking and feeling. You can read quite a lot from people's faces. Congruent and incongruent signals and expressions show whether somebody stands for what he's saying. But always check and, moreover, always ask whether your conclusion is the right one. A thoughtful face may look very serious and angry, while there is no anger at all.

The expressions of the eye, with the minimal differences in the surrounding landscape of the muscles of the eye, give away a lot of information. Eyes withdrawn into the eye socket, open and smiling eyes, pensive eyes, eyes in a trance and in an unreachable place, inviting eyes. Also the voice has its variables: the rhythm, the volume, the tone, the vitality and directness strongly determine how a message will be heard. Those variables are clearly recognizable signals in communication. They quickly lead to determinations and judgments! Your voice can sound angry, impatient, sad, happy, pushy, nagging, etc.

The movements of arms and hands can also show how someone feels. The unmoving and emotionless speaker or the opposite, the enthusiastic speaker with many supporting movements of arms, hands and whole body, are quite different postures. Movements can highlight the message. Think about the commanding forefinger knocking on the table desk as a supportive gesture for "I warn you for …. and remember that ….".

You can also conclude things from someone's posture. Closed arms, legs, looking away from the other, emphatic looking at you, and so on. We're inclined to give a meaning to such postures. Closed arms seem to be a kind of self-protection and being inaccessible, crossed legs seem to tell: till here and no further, I won't let you 'touch' me. Turning away from the other seems to be indifferent and really not wanting any contact or even breaking the contact. An emphatic and persisting look seems to tell: "don't you dare to have a different opinion". And of course, there are always moments that all those quick judgments are true, but always check them. Be aware that the closed arms could also be a comfortable posture, the turning away may be just a moment to consider or to process what has been said and the persisting look may be a sign of super fascination.

Non-verbal signals have an obvious reinforcing effect in communication. Research shows that the meaning of your communication is formed by what you say, for only a small part (7%). Much more important is the body language and posture, facial expression and voice variables (such as volume, tone and speed). But check them. And you'll find that if you're right that there were several signs that express and confirm the same. It was also to be heard in the voice, the facial expression also matched, just like the expression of the eyes. When those things occur at the same time, we say the "cluster effect in non-verbal signals" connect and support the outspoken text and makes it to a (in)congruent expression.

1.6 The use of I or YOU messages [3]

Thomas Gordon, author of many books about relationships (with children, adults and business) indicates the use of "YOU messages" as very disruptive. Especially the use of it in feedback messages or discussions, very often causes the creation of an unpleasant atmosphere. People feel misunderstood, feel offended and try to correct or defend themselves.

The Gordon method is based on equality in relations, the willingness to take responsibility for a relation, while taking into account the other. Besides active listening (listening, summarizing and further asking in a state with all attention to the other) proves the use of I-messages in communication to be a constructive one.

I-message doesn't accuse like the YOU-message.

By using I-messages you give expression to your own needs, desires, opinions without condemning or blaming the other.

An I-message ideally contains:
• a description or reference to the behavior why feedback is given (and has striking similarities to be discussed with the G-model feedback);
• the feeling what has been triggered;
• the result and impact of it.

In the spoken language the I-messages are used in a much faster way. The

---

[3]Thomas Gordon, leadership effectivity training

---

three parts (description – triggered feeling – impact) are knitted together, but still present:

- when I'm tired I don't want to ... ... (... refers to the behavior on which the feedback is given; 'feeling tired' and 'don't want to' refers to the wanted result i.e. 'not going');

- I would like to work quietly (quietly refers to 'now it appears not to be quiet', the feeling is mentioned by 'like' and the request by the words 'I want'.

The use of 'you-messages' in discussions isn't a useful one, because they are easily interpreted as accusing or compelling. A You-message almost always starts with the word YOU.

A 'you-message' seems to force responsibility, like:

-you must stop, (because .... and why don't you!)

-you want all the attention, (which is annoying and why do you act like that?)

-you shouldn't do that (and because you know that, why are you doing it anyway?)

1.7 Compare the impact of an I- and a You -message

Just giving clear messages isn't that easy. Practicing it is necessary and you'll discover an increasingly fast use of it. A pitfall is the combination of I and YOU messages together. "I think you ... ',' I want you ....", "I hope you ....", "I like it when you..." are some example expressions of this combination. They all start with an unfinished I-message followed by a YOU message.

I-message	YOU-message
I don't want to go out, because I'm too tired.	You should stop asking whether I want to go out, because I'm too tired.
I would like to really talk together about this subject.	I don't like it when you keep on interrupting me.
I can't work in such an environment.	You make such a noise, I can't work anymore
I prefer working in an undisturbed way.	You shouldn't disturb me when I'm busy.
I want to continue for a moment.	You have to wait.
I don't like this.	You are annoying when doing so!
I think it's hard to talk about this right now.	I don't want you to force me talking about that right now.

1.8 'Wrong' messages

> *It is much clearer to say precisely what you do want,*
> *than keep on telling what you don't want over and over again.*

Thomas Gordon describes a range of nine categories of 'wrong messages' that are easily used in discussions. All these expressions make the recipient feel uncomfortable or cause difficulty to remain in a neutral state, or to stay in a non-defensive attitude.

• Give orders, directions or commanding

    o Do something else

    o Stop it, you destroy ....

    o Put that back.

• To warn, admonish, threaten

    o If you do not stop, then I ...

    o I get angry when you continue ...

    o If you do not provide ... .. then ....

• Preaching, moralize

    o You should not disturb anyone when he ....

    o You can't do that because ....

    o You should always ensure that ... ..

• Council, give suggestions or solutions

    o Why don't you ... ..?

    o I will think of something else for you

    o Can't you do...... when you do this?

• Give judgments, criticize and accuse

- o You should have known better
- o You're boring
- o I get sick of you
- Insults, ridiculizing, shame
  - o You are a quite boring someone
  - o Now it's enough
  - o You ought to be ashamed!
- Interpreting, determine causes, analyzing
  - o You just want attention
  - o You're trying to rattle me
  - o I know what you're trying to
- To know it all & better, give instructions
  - o Decent people do not….
  - o How would you feel if I say to you…..
  - o I told you already to do so…
- Insinuate
  - o Probably you are just trying to ……
  - o I think you want him to blame him for the failure of the project.

All these messages suggest (or order) what another person shouldn't do. All messages are given in a vague way. The communication would be much clearer if you let the other person exactly know what you really want. Saying what you want at the same time implies things you do not want. Not necessarily mentioning them explicitly. The advantage is that the other person can immediately focus on what you want and he simultaneously receives neutral feedback about his behavior.

2

MAKE IT EASIER

This chapter gives you extra tips & tricks to increase your ability to give feedback in a right way or moment, but also to improve the content.

2.1   Introduction

Couldn't you say that in a different way!

I haven't said that!

Say what you want to say!

These phrases express very clearly that there are differences in the way a person makes or receives comments. People are so different. Person A will say something to B and assumes it has been said in a neat and clear way, but the other one labels it as confronting, maybe rude and without compassion and thus causing misunderstandings or bad feelings as a result of the confrontation. But what is confronting? We'll see that there are objective differences in the way we can describe confrontations:

- Tips, the gentlest form. "You know what you could try in this ... is... ... ... ". You give a message or an idea to the other so he can decide to apply it or not;

- The (collegiate) designation, the command. Short and concise, without emotions, just like an instruction. Not acting difficult, just do and run. Works great in an environment where this skill is mutually respected.

- Feedback, targeted at anyone attempting him to move to different behavior. Your goal is to help the other person to change his behavior, so you have less problems with it. Or you want something to be better executed than it is done now. Feedback is always purposeful. The situation which you're in, or what you want to achieve determines the method how you give the feedback. In this book we describe four different methods and applications.

- Criticism, the feedback phase is passed. You're sick of that continuing behavior, or you have no other possibilities in that situation. Criticism is much more confronting than feedback. It is definite. You think (!) the other is doing things in the wrong way. No discussions about it, it should be stopped, period! In the way critics are given, there are big differences, like being constructive, neutral, emotional or destructive. The constructive way is pretty much like feedback, but more directive.

- Correcting someone in a direct way and pointing out that things must change, for better or for worse. Something has to change! This can only be applied in a satisfactory manner as it is immediately clear what the correction delivers in a positive way. What disadvantages are eliminated and what benefits are achieved? A simple order to do it in this way will not be appreciated by anyone and will lead to dissatisfaction and opposition.

- With the blunt instrument through it. An emotional expression, with destructive characteristics and often caused by anger or despair. Not knowing (anymore) how to approach that person in a constructive way to realize changes in behavior. Angriness or despair often caused by repeated disappointments and humiliations. Relationships are harmed and tend to be harmed even more. You may ask whether you should continue this cooperation or quit. Destructive emotions affect not only others, but also yourself.

2.2 First understand before being understood

How to give feedback is the main thrust of this book. Less attention is paid to receiving feedback. This is because the way you receive feedback in almost all cases is the same as giving feedback. The main difference is that you're standing on the other side. Everything you want to achieve with giving good feedback and you're hoping for, is a pleasant, open and constructive reaction. In receiving feedback, that's the thing that is asked from you.

And as you have experienced many times by yourself: it's not easy. Especially when it's related to critical feedback that triggers your emotions. You can hear yourself say: "Well, yes, I might be wrong according to you, but maybe you should take more time for your observations, I don't like the way you say that, it's really different compared to what you think." Defense as the first response. And as you know, many people fall back on their own opinions, own criteria and judge the other and perceive further information in a filtered way. The fight can begin!

Receiving feedback could be a whole lot easier when you use the motto:

"first understand others and then try to be understood".

Listen, hear and understand. What are the reasons why the other person says something about you or your behavior? Behind all the feedback there's an implicit question: "can you act differently?" What should be different and how do you think he means and wants that? Behind his remarks is a real sense, which is constrained. Would you leave it that way or are you willing to help the other and to ensure that there remains a fine or good relationship? Ask questions addressed to the other to understand and identify what he requests you to focus on.

Be willing to listen. Agreement isn't necessary at that moment (at least not yet), just get information to understand the other.

Ask yourself:

- What exactly is his problem?
- What is the need he's struggling with and needs to be fulfilled?
- What was the cause? How did you cause that (unintentionally)? Why could it be that he draws conclusions in this way?

Be open and respect the other. If you think you really understand the other, then start with your story. Also (and foremost) respect yourself and go in a conversation with him about your arguments, about your needs and your feelings. If you expect feedback and you know feedback could be useful, you make it a whole lot easier to invite the other to give feedback. "I want to know what you think about ……." Through your openness, you create openness, you probably take stress away and bring the other in a more neutral state to give the feedback in a useful, constructive way.

2.3 Yes-but, Yes-and and No-because[4]

• Use 'Yes-and' if you have a different opinion or insight. By using 'yes-and' your language becomes much more constructive. People may have different opinions, insights and arguments. Treating them with a "but….." suggests a denial. Yes-but is equal to No; no-but is equal to Yes. Those words cause tension, cause a feeling of rejection because you immediately refer to your point of view instead of showing recognition. The 'Yes-And' way respects the opinion of the other (yes) and gives space for yours (and). This step will much quicker lead to a nicer conversation and can continue with how do we find a solution?

• Use 'No-because' when you have arguments with which you can strongly support your opinion. You may have the knowledge on which you base your opinions.

• Use only 'Yes-but' when you critically examine, analyze, discuss and exchange statements. For the rest: limit the use of the 'yes-but's'. Because a yes-but means no! The 'Yes-butter' is nagging, denying, pretending to know the truth, isn't choosing, is unclear, is mismatching, most times he's more problem-focused than solution-oriented.

---

[4] Based on Berthold Gunster's: Yes-but what if it all works out?

2.4 Compliments & Appreciation

Receiving compliments and appreciation seems to be very easy. But that isn't the case. When a compliment is received, people often react with a rejecting gesture or remark. "No, no thanks", "that's obvious" or "oh, that's part of my task and therefore you don't have to compliment me" or "I'm getting paid for it." Rejections made in many different ways. But the pitfall is inherent. And that's too bad, because the rejection of the received appreciation isn't really incorporated and causes the thought: "Ah, yes, maybe he's right."

Sometimes it even looks like we're not able to receive a nice compliment anymore and instead easily come in a denial mood, sending a message that positive feedback isn't necessary. The next time you really need that pat on the back, there probably won't come any.

And perhaps continuous rejection of compliments leads to how we become dull. A work environment wherein giving and receiving compliments isn't present anymore will be a boring environment. And in the long run we'll all miss such little rewards. Then we all start complaining toward the management. "They only see mistakes, but if you perform in the right way it isn't recognized." The criticism you hear will be overly present. "You never get to hear something positive, not even a gesture. How small." When no (longer) compliments are given, they will be missed and suddenly the need for it increases to a disproportionate size.

Another effect of the rejected compliments or appreciation is that we no longer make contact with the joy and the pleasure it delivers. A pleasure that can bring you an every day party by celebrating those little 'successes'. The only thing you have to do is recognize it and reward yourself. Appreciate positive feedback, give yourself 'party time' at such a moment and reply to the other with a positive remark.

Another situation in which compliments should be given is when people walk around with uncertainties. The giving and receiving of feedback in those cases is really important. It increases self-confidence, it takes away doubts, it makes your day superb and as a bonus: you can learn from it. It provides a great feeling. Give it a try and give people an unexpected compliment for example when you've been served well in a shop or on the phone.

The reaction will be visible. Smiling faces are then followed by "oh yes nice to hear that ☺, or… well sir that is how I'm supposed to do ☺.

Cherish positive feedback, and receive it with open arms. Hang the garlands by yourselves, celebrate your party and next give truly sincere compliments to others.

2.5 The observation positions

To provide feedback it's necessary to have or to gather information about how to treat a discussion with someone else. All this information is gathered by yourself, pretending as if you look from a different point of view to the relation. (And of course you can also receive good advices from somebody else, sometimes you just have to ask for it.)

You can do this exercise really spatial. In the different steps of the model you receive more information out of four perspectives. Use that information in the center spot as if you would receive it in reality.

• 1   Move up the **other**, look at the discussion and relation through his eyes. You really try to picture that. This usually provides surprising information. What would he advise you to do, to have the best effect? How would he advise (i.e. feedback) how you create the best state in communicating with him? Honor and use that information. Of course it's still information you created. But you could create this because you probably already knew the other much longer than just that particular moment. So you

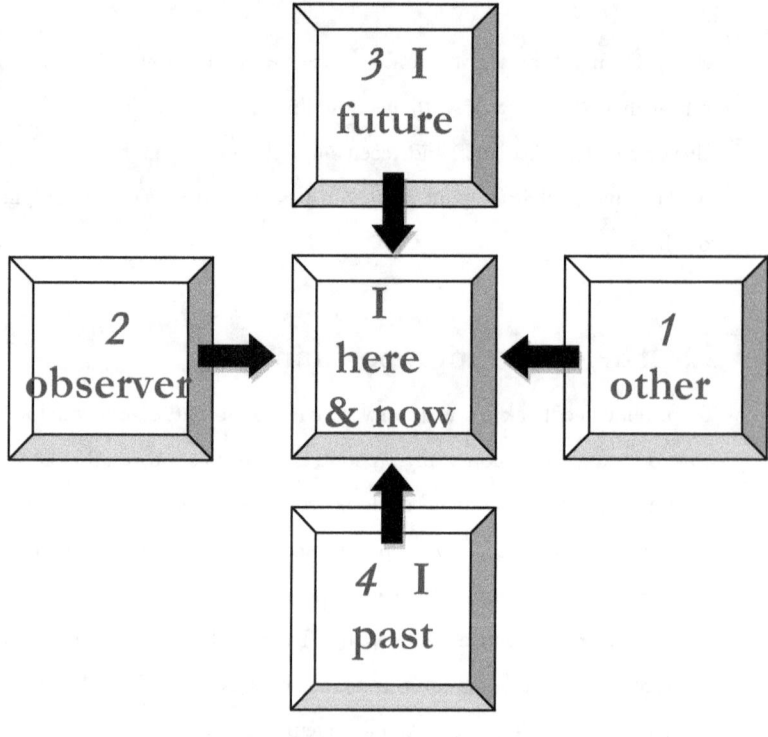

Model of the observation positions

have information about his style, his criteria and his concerns. Use it.

When feelings and emotion are playing a solid and disturbing role in providing feedback, it's useful to step back in that position and create a more rational considering state.

- 2 Imagine you're a neutral **observer**, just a passenger. See the problem or case in the relation with the other, as if you look through the eyes of the neutral and not involved observer. As if you're passing by those two people, seeing and hearing the discussion. What would that observer advise you from his perspective? Ask yourself again whether it's worth it and how you could apply that information to discuss better?

Actually if you just create another neutral point of view to the problem, it immediately neutralizes your emotions. Due to that you can respond in a more rational way.

- 3 the **future**

People right in the middle of a conflict tend to be narrow minded. All they see and hear is judged by their then present and important criteria. It's really amazing how often people make different judgments just a day or a week later. How could I be so stubborn, how could I be so confronting, I should have listened better, aaaaahh that's really not worth such a verbal fight. So move up to a point in the future. Imagine that a year has passed and you judge that conflict or discussion again. What advice would you give to the 'I' in the present position? What behavior would contribute in a more positive way to the discussion? It's also another way to create distance to the present feeling.

• 4   lessons from the **past**

It's also a well known phenomenon that emotions disturb the clean and reliable use of former lessons learned. Often you already have the information, but your memory is stuck as a result of these emotions.

Take a step back in history, in your past. Search an identical discussion or conflict. Question yourself what you actually did in that situation, or what you learned about that for future use. Could this information also be useful for the present case? For the whole case or for only a part? If yes, use it. Sometimes it even appears people have the ability to use "the lessons learned by other people."

2.6 General feedback rules

Make sure feedback is

• Focused on the behavior and not on the person,

• Descriptive, not judgmental,

• Specific and not general

• A personal observation and not an interpretation or based on information from others,

• Considering the feelings of the feedback giver as well as the receiver,

• Right in time and

• Useful for the recipient.

2.7 Tips for giving feedback

* Agree to disagree. Honor the presupposition that you both may disagree.
* Speak in 'I-messages'. In doing so, you just say what happens to you and at the same time you make it possible for the other to understand what's going on with you.
* Be clear, detailed and unambiguous.
* Do not exaggerate and stick to reality.
* Do not condemn and leave words like good, better, bad, belongs to, really behind.
* Speak for yourself, not on behalf of others or based on information from others.
* Talk about yourself first, not about the other. So I .....
* Restrict yourself to the things that you know, or observed by yourself.
* Describe what the effect of the behavior of the other means to you.
* Describe the feedback very pointed and directly. Avoid general terms, if people....., the department ...., the others ... .
* Respect reactions as they are.

2.8 Tips for receiving feedback

* Agree to disagree. Again honor the presupposition that you both may disagree once again.

- Take a deep breath, up to and including the belly. Our body tends to react to tensed situations like a physical attack and in a response to that we start fast and shallow breathing. Correct yourself.
- Listen carefully and do not interrupt.
- Ask yourself what the needs of the feedback giver could be.
- Ask questions for clarification.
- Show you noticed and understood the feedback and repeat what you heard in your own words.
- Recognize and respect legitimate points. Agree with what is true and acknowledge what is possible. Take time to think about what you've heard. Ask questions till you've comprehended everything.
- First: perceive,
  second: consider,
  third: judge.

2.9 How to screw up feedback

- Speak in YOU messages.
  You've .... and you did ...... and enlarge the feeling of being accused. With this the defense immediately starts.
- Condemn.
- Confuse feedback with competence (playing the win & loose game).
- Use feedback based on assumptions and just thinking that...., instead of based on verified facts,
- Provide feedback with a negative attitude.
- Be too late.

- Give feedback while you're still angry.

- Give feedback without taking care of the other.

- Ask questions such as why did you ...., make him accountable for...

- Avoid giving the opportunity to the other to reply.

2.10   Security in a group

An important condition for feedback is security.

Within a team (and evidently in every relationship), safety is a condition before giving critical feedback. This requires a major leadership role.

Although each employee also has a co-responsibility, there's an explicit task (and role model) for every manager or supervisor.

We all know and recognize that there are a number of negative scenarios that highly influence this security.

- When it's likely that you are squared up later (which can happen in very subtle ways) then there's a lack of security and then better don't supply feedback. Nobody does.

- Getting a big mouth from a colleague what is not been corrected later on by his supervisor creates a tense and unsafe atmosphere.

- Wise guys colleagues have a covered attitude and create inaccessibility. They aren't open and repeal a real conversation. The manager or supervisor should create conditions to ensure that everyone can go in conversation with anyone about anything. Quality of work requires this.

- The manager or supervisor with a changing attitude to feedback. Alternatively he promotes feedback and then not. Or has friends who get preferential treatment and victims who are always doomed.

- The supervisor who listens more to complaining customers instead of neutral investigating the incident and thus accusing the employee.

- The executive who doesn't remove the rotten apples in a team, spoils the whole barrel. Why should you then give feedback anyway? Only quarrels appear and are not corrected.

- The executive who doesn't make result-oriented and specific agreements with his employees, will not achieve big changes.

- The executive who attaches more importance to financial management rather than people management creates a fighting work environment.

- The executive who isn't able to work with feedback by himself, both giving and receiving, is someone not to be trusted. He's a bad role model.

The manager has a crucial role in building safety and openness as a condition to give feedback within a team. He's the director of how people interact. He monitors all activities and takes care of continuity.

He charges, he facilitates, he controls, he coaches and he corrects. He uses many management tools to succeed, like performance appraisals, team meetings, managing by walking around and personal interviews.

If these processes run well, you can and should expect from each employee involved that he also takes responsibility for the team processes.

3

FEEDBACK

3.1 Introduction

1. The BEIR-model (Behavior – Emotion – Impact – Request)

2. Feedback with compassion by Marshall Rosenberg

3. Learning Feedback, Tips & Tops

4. Feedback Solution Focused, including appreciative feedback

5. Harm causing feedback

These feedback methods (except the harm causing) have a common theme: the dialogue should be initiated. Only through dialogue there will be a real conversation with exchanging information between people. If this happens you can decide whatever you want to do with that information.

Words like you must, you should, you have to, you will, you can't… all include an obliging tendency and cause resistance. People want to make choices for themselves, freely.

Providing feedback means that there's another person who receives the feedback. The intention is to give that person so much specific information that he's willing to think about it and inquires what worth or insights it provides to him. And of course you hope that the other person adjusts his behavior so your feedback creates the wanted results.

And of course because you have a wanted result you give the feedback. And you have to give the feedback in such a way that it doesn't cause a defensive attitude, and you're allowed to give feedback. It should lead to an open attitude wherein the other is really wondering what is exactly said and asked. The feedback receiver considers the value of the feedback, what is expected to be changed, what can be in it for me if I change, does it contributes to my own needs etcetera? How should I take responsibility for improvement in a win-win process? Only when this succeeds and you get to a conversation both of you will learn and grow.

This also applies for receiving feedback. Be open-minded and leave all defensive behavior behind. Consider what the other says and wants, even invite him as much as possible to give as much feedback as possible to get information. Find out what you can learn, what it can deliver for you, how the feedback is like a gift for you instead of considering it as an annoying remark.

Invite others to tell their opinion and show & tell them you're open minded and even want to learn from their information. The invitation to provide the feedback will elicit that and facilitates a possible dialogue.

The four methods presented here will, when properly applied, deliver those results.

3.2 The BEIR-model

Step 1   DESCRIBE THE **B**EHAVIOR

Describe what you see / saw, hear / heard, note / noticed.

This is what you observe, without judging it.

I see you do... ... ...

and meanwhile I heard you say that ... ...

Step 2   DESCRIBE THE **E**MOTIONS & FEELINGS

Identify what the behavior in step 1 elicits. You want to say something about it, because it evokes a feeling, an emotion (can be both negative and positive). That emotion or feeling is the real reason for your feedback.

And so I get the feeling ... ...

Step 3   DESCRIBE THE **I**MPACT OF THE EMOTIONS

Due to this emotion & feeling ... ... (step 2) it results in an impact on you or this relationship. Identify the impact on you and the impact on the interaction between you and the other.

And the result is that I ... ...

Step 4   **R**EQUEST   AND   ASK   WHAT   YOU   NEED   TO   NEUTRALIZE   THE EMOTION/FEELING AGAIN

This impact (step 3) means that you want to ask the other person to behave in a specific or different way. That's your need you want to be clear about.

I would therefore appreciate it if you ... ...

With a simple addition to these four steps you can define an even clearer result:

All right? Can we agree? Can we make this to an appointment?

You create a more compelling step when you add:

And what do you propose to do when you relapse again in the old behavior or habit?

This last addition is about sanctions and unpleasant consequences. The responsibility for this step should be with the other person (you just ask him about the consequences). Asking this question and getting an answer on it, makes a correction in a later phase a lot easier. And of course you only add this step when it concerns somebody who 'easily' forgets appointments and 'easily' relapses into the old pattern. This happens mostly due to a real lack of motivation to change. Of course the effectuating step is to execute the self-chosen sanction, otherwise you'll never be taken serious again.

> **A little sincerity is a dangerous thing,**
>
> **and a great deal of it is absolutely fatal.**
>
> *Oscar Wilde, Irish dramatist, novelist, & poet (1854 - 1900)*

Application

In the ordinary everyday communication like colleagues amongst each other, partners in a relationship or parents with their children. Are emotions getting stronger, is the dispute a serious conflict, then the approach of Marshall Rosenberg is more appropriate.

Copy the feedback note on the next page, so you can practice with the model. You'll notice that you sometimes merge step 2 & 3, or turn them around in order, sometimes even omit step 2. This is all right as long as you notice that your feedback has been understood and the other person reacts in an appropriate way. If confusion occurs, you better evaluate if you have applied and completed all the steps in the right way.

3.3 The BEIR feedback note

Use the feedback note to prepare for an interview.

If you repeat the four steps, you'll learn the skill much faster. Feedback just by giving this note feedback is 'not-done'. Let it always be followed with a conversation.

B E I R

From ... ... To ... ...

1. DESCRIBE THE **B**EHAVIOR

    "I see, I saw, I hear, I hear, I see, it strikes me that ....

    ... ...

    ... ... "

2. DESCRIBE THE **E**MOTIONS & FEELINGS

    "And so I get the feeling ... ...

    ... ...

    ... . "

3. DESCRIBE THE **I**MPACT OF THE EMOTIONS

    And thus/as a result or effect caused by that emotion I ... ...

    .. ..

    ... ... "

4. **R**EQUEST AND ASKED WHAT YOU NEED TO NEUTRALIZE THE EMOTION & FEELING AGAIN

    And I would appreciate it if you ... ...

    ... ...

    ... ... "

5. Facultative

AND THE AGREEMENT IS... ....
... ...
... ...
... ..

6. Facultative

AND WHAT DO YOU PROPOSE TO DO WHEN YOU RELAPSE
AGAIN IN THE OLD BEHAVIOR OR HABIT? ... ...
... ...
... ...
... ...
... ...
... ...

3.4 Feedback with compassion

(Derived from Marshall Rosenberg's nonviolent communication)

An observation stimulates one or more feelings. Becoming aware of feelings makes clear what need(s) have been fulfilled or unfulfilled. Then we can choose for action (request). If we are truly curious and wondering from which feelings and need(s) we communicate with others, then we draw from our natural source of contributions to space for all life. Both in ourselves and in others around us[5].

The BEIR-model could have been derived from the non-violent communication. The main difference is that Rosenberg is strongly focused on pure perception and omits judgments entirely. Followed by the challenge to identify the present emotions and feelings and the underlying and accompanying needs that cause these emotions. The last step is therefore a question or making a request in that direction to solve the tension.

3.4.1 Introduction

Because Rosenberg goes much deeper than the BEIR-model it is very suitable in conflict situations. Conflicts in which previous feedback and criticism didn't have the expected results and led to a greater personal distance instead of a better understanding of each other. Or in situations where there are such strong emotions like sadness, grief, hurt or feeling offended playing a disturbing role and you still want to get into a serious

---

[5] Authenta 2008, part of "the model of non violent communication", page 32

conversation.

The great value of Rosenberg's approach is the increase of understanding of each other. When we have disagreements we evolve to a situation where we can accept that parties have their own opinion and that willingness is needed to see the bigger picture. This usually shows that

1.   there's a recognition of the problem of the other

2.   there's agreement about and recognition of the right to have own point of views, own opinions, own needs and feelings. For each person involved in the conflict.

3.   the sense of equality will be created again, much faster and with a lot more respect for individual diversity.

In very emotional and sensitive situations it is really the same process. Recognize the emotion of the other, give him the right to have his emotion, even when you don't like that emotion. Investigate and ask what the underlying need could be, that causes that emotion.

Rosenberg devotes much attention to the decoupling of perception and judgments. And that's pretty hard, because we learned the skill of judging since childhood. We are raised with right and wrong, in many variations. Quick judging is sometimes even considered a great quality. And of course a doctor or fire fighter must quickly judge. Only in communication, including feedback, it's a disadvantage rather than an advantage.

3.4.2 Judging & perceiving

There is something more to be said about judging. Judging itself is OK. As already said, in many professions you are often expected to decide very quickly. And of course, the process of making good decisions heavily relies on the ability of judging. This part, the internal part and fully focused on

your internal process in the mind is the judging part everybody needs. Also in another way it's very useful to judge very quickly. All signals you're aware of in the relations and communication between people surrounding you, will create a sense of safety. Related to people it's a skill to not be naive. It would be stupid to ignore those signals and not to investigate them. And one of the major things the human body will do, is taking care of its own safety. It better does! That process is also based on judgments and that's OK too.

But if the judging process is directed outwards, to other people, to the things people say or do in specific situations we should be more careful. We're still not able to read other people's minds. Most times we don't know what processes people are in, what thoughts they have, what feelings they experience, what concerns, what sorrows, what values people have, what spirituality they relate to. In judging related to those things we should be more careful.

3.4.3   The Steps

> *"You only can be free and happy when you fully take the responsibility for your own".*
> *Josef Kirschner*

Step 1 COMPASSION

Always be compassionate, come close and relate to the other with compassion, with real curiosity, and mercy. In the same way as you show compassion for yourself. Only by taking care of your own, you'll be able to take care and be valuable and compassionate for others.

Empathy consists of awareness, involvement, openness, nearness, empathy, compassion, warmth, respect, kindness / tenderness, brightness. Compassion means that you are both in touch with yourself and with others. That you're open to the feelings of yourself as to the feelings of others. The allowance of those feelings to be there, without judgment. Compassion means that you listen to the story of the other without looking for agreement or disagreement.

Compassion leads to a way of listening that implies both empathy and sympathy. Empathy implies that you try to see through the eyes, to hear through the ears, to feel through all senses of the other what they may feel and experience. Empathy means that you recognize and focus on the emotions and feelings and continue to communicate with full respect to those emotions and feelings. In addition, it could be that there are other feelings being stimulated. Compassion is an attitude, is a state in which you simultaneously are with the other and with yourself. Compassion is a connection in the here and now with the self and other, and creates respect and harmony.[6]

---

[6] Authenta 2008, part of "the model of non violent communication", page 41

This is a basic attitude or state. Even when it's hard to do, just try to experience the other with compassion. You'll discover a new world, even in an annoying moment. Why does he hate you? What is it what's irritating him? What does he really want you to do? Questions that will be answered if you're willing to look, to listen and to feel with compassion in the next four steps.

Step 2 PERCEIVE

Everything you see, hear, smell, taste or feel is a perception. To perceive is everything your senses notice. Sheer expression without any interpretation or opinion.

- *I see, I saw, I hear, I heard so, I notice on ... ...*
  ... ...

Step 3 CHECK THE FEELING

Ask yourself what the feeling or emotion could be why he's behaving like that (what you perceive in step 1). Ask for it or guess it and verify the correctness.

- *I wonder what you feel at this moment, because I'd like to understand you*
- *And I think you're sad about what happens, is that right?*

Step 4 WHAT ARE THE NEEDS?

And since feelings are based on needs, there's always an (expected) unsatisfied need that causes this feeling or emotion. This presupposition ensures that step 3 occurs and is made perceptible in step 2. If that need is recognized and told, the other one will sense a feeling of being taken seriously.

Try to be able to see further than (the end of) one's nose, looking beyond your own interests or concerns only. This often leads to an opening for a more constructive conversation.

- *I wonder what the reasons are or what your needs are, why I obviously provoke that emotion when I call you?*
- *I want to know your underlying needs, so I can make up my mind and see if I can do anything for you.*

Step 5 THE REQUEST

- *So I ask you to tell me this, so I understand what matters to you.*
- *Would you like to tell me what is important for you?*

This way of expressing very quickly changes into a smooth style if practiced regularly and will be more powerful when expressed in your own words.

3.4.4 Pitfalls for each step

Pitfall: perceive

We are accustomed to the blending of perception and interpretation. Usually followed by an assessment. Then we consider this interpretation as the only correct opinion.

I think that ... ... followed by an interpretation / judgment of the behavior you see from the other. We could also check whether our interpretation is consistent and the same with that of the other person:

I have the feeling that ... . Is that right? How is that for you?

Pitfall: claims and assertions

Someone is ... ., or something is ... ...

Claims are identified by the use of the verb "to be". Claims are assumptions (usually) based on too little information. Sometimes people just state something and then talk about it as if it's real, without further verification.

Assertions may be challenged by a series of four questions.

For example: He is very critical.

- *How do you know?*
- *How do you know this is true?*
- *Imagine that it is wrong, then how wrong was that assumption / assertion before?*
- *And imagine if another would say that about you!*

We better only rely on what we see, hear, smell, taste or feel. And whenever you think that......... ... . Ask!

Pitfall: check the feeling and emotions!

The denial of responsibility for your own feelings confuses many discussions. And if you think you're not responsible, then the only possibility is to blame the other for that feeling. Annoying situations arise where feelings are expressed and the other is declared guilty.

I feel .... because you ... ...

It would be much better to show responsibility for your own feelings, as the result of something happening to you or something missing. Your need has not been fulfilled.

I feel bad because I really preferred going home much earlier, instead of : *I feel bad because you didn't let me go earlier.*

A tricky one is talking about feelings or emotions, the so-called quasi feelings, or meta-talk. Not the real feeling or emotion is appointed but just what you think you feel.

I feel ignored, I think I feel angriness; I don't feel comfortable with this action. Genuine and real expressions of feelings are composed with the verb to be. They are so clear and honest:

I'm confused, I'm angry, I'm happy, I'm upset.

Pitfall: what are the needs?

The way how a need is realized is a strategy. For example: to work in a pleasant way you want nice colleagues and respectful communication. Needs and how they are established (the strategy) are easily confused. In the example the strategies are: 1. the selection of nice colleagues (need = pleasure) and 2. the demonstrated respectful communication (need = openness, integrity, cooperation, getting elbow-room). And of course there are many ways (= strategies) to select new colleagues and how to work together. There are more strategies possible to accomplish a single need. Be careful with mixing up strategies and needs.

Sometimes we go too far, a strategy becomes a habit and a habit becomes an addiction or compulsive behavior. An example: think of someone who's not able to solve his problem on his own (his need: the problem should disappear and feeling good). At one point he receives the support of somebody, a bit of practical help. That worked so well that he decides to ask for help again and again. The dependency increases and he doesn't learn to solve his problems without external help. The need = solve the problem, the strategy = asking for help. It's good to be aware that there is a difference between real needs and the way that you fulfill them. The real need in a discussion is much more important than the strategy how to solve the need. It shows something about your personality.

Needs become really oppressing when they are linked to specific people only. You want that person to be around, he or she should do something to make you feel good and has to co-build your world in such a way you feel comfortable. Dependency is the result. Both you and the other should say no to misplaced responsibility.

Pitfall: the request

A request is a true request when it can be answered with an honest no, without any unpleasant reaction afterwards. A refusal, a no, even an annoying rejection, it must be possible to say. Isn't that the case then there's no real free choice. Even subtle placed demands turn out to be oppressed questions.

A request should also be a question that encourages action. This is the reason why unfree questions are experienced as very uncomfortable. The recipient should do things he didn't choose for. Check for yourself what the words "you should", "you must", "you have no other choice" trigger.

- Requiring: a Yes, an OK is the only possible answer.

    This equates with an order or command.

- Blackmailing: if you don't do what I ask, then ... ...

    The punishment is already announced.

- Asking confusing questions: when it's unclear what exactly is the request, or to whom exactly it was directed, formulated in a negative or double negative way, or without a precise time frame this request was placed in.

Pitfall: compassion

Most of us have learned not to ask directly for what we want. Waiting for one's turn is the device at school when children ask questions. Not asking means that we give away our responsibility for our wellbeing. Often we hope, believe and expect that the other person just knows what we want or need. And when we get disappointed, we're not understood and the desired action won't come, then we are hurt or angry. The manifestation of the anger or feeling of hurt cause (after a moment of self reflection) a reaction of fear, guilt or shame and we end up in a vicious circle[7].

The pitfall here is that we often deliver unasked consolation, advices and solutions. We take over their story, make their experience less important, deny or even downplay (ah, you don't have to feel like that). Such a feedback just shows the trouble you have yourself with the situation. Often you just want to have a "normal relationship without tension" with each other. Acting that way will probably ensure that both won't learn anything of the situation and the problem will come back a next time for sure.

Marshal Rosenberg's nonviolent communication method is a nice way to approach difficult and emotional situations. Especially the showing of compassion leads to thawing of these problematic situations.

---

[7] Authenta 2008, part of "the model of non violent communication", page 40-41

3.4.5 Examples

Example of obtrusive behavior from Mike to Henri.

Henri suffers from Mike's obtrusiveness, which causes a lot of irritations. Due to Mike's obtrusive behavior Henri's need to finally solve his own problems is stressed. In Rosenbergs' method, Henri's irritation is replaced and turned over in a more positive "engaged, understanding, serious, respect and compassion showing"-state for Mike. Because Mike has shown in his conduct that he apparently has a reason (doesn't matter whether that reason is right or wrong) to behave obtrusive. Apparently he wants to fulfill his own needs. Henri may say to Mike that he really wants to understand the reasons why Mike wants to help so quickly. But also he wants to explain how he feels receiving this unasked help, which emotions are triggered at the same time and which personal need isn't met in such a situation. Then Henri could say how Mike can do better. Followed by asking Mike if he (Henri) should improve or change something in his own communication to get a better understanding?

Probably the negative interference between them will disappear and there's enough space for a real conversation and understanding.

Example oncology: the conversation with an angry mother.

A mother is upset and angry about the seemingly indifferent way nurses talk about 'cases' with each other. She has picked up such a conversation unexpectedly when she walked into the staff room. Her child with a tumor is one of those 'cases'.

Nurse: I hear you say you are angry about the 'clean' way we talk about the care or the medical examination of our patients in our profession. I understand that you don't like the way we talk about it? Is that what you mean madam?

Mrs. will then probably respond that it sounds so impersonal and so cold how they confer and discuss together. Hearing that as a mother is painful and embarrassing to accept. A very ill child is not a case!

Nurse can then respond by saying: if I understand you well you would prefer that we talk in a much more sympathetic and polite manner about our patients so you don't need to get upset anymore. Madam: I would like that!

Example nursing: communication about an Alzheimer's patient.

The family was very surprised not to meet their mom in her room. They already had some discussions about this with the nursing staff and talked about security and the desirability that mother shouldn't wander around on the ward, because of the possibility she may "escape". Yet this still happens again and again.

Family: Mother is gone again, despite all the arrangements we made. I blame you all that this happens again and again. If things go wrong I will officially submit a report about it!

Nursing: Mrs. I see and notice that you're really angry, after all those discussions and arrangements you expected your mother wouldn't be able to leave her room without guidance anymore.

Family: yes of course. Otherwise, what else would we make arrangements for? You'd better be careful and implement these arrangements.

Nursing: I understand. Every time this happens you get more worried, caused by the earlier made arrangements not being met. So your reassurance disappears and you feel quite uncomfortable with the situation.

Family: Yes of course, what else would you expect?

Nurse: How can we ensure you that we intend to hold on to these arrangements we made? We can't stay in the room literally all the time due to understaffing. Do you have any ideas on how we could meet your needs in a better way? Because we also think that mom benefits when you are present in a pleasant way when you're visiting her.

Family: Yes, of course, that's why we are so upset and angry!

Nursing: We certainly want to cooperate with you. What do you think could be more contributing to the security of your mother besides the "room strategy"? And not only for your mom, but also on your feeling that the desired security is really thought about and offered, at least that the intention to do so is present. We find it important that you are satisfied and we would like it if you think together with us about better solutions. We would be glad if you'd help us with this serious problem.

The family will now probably raise constructive alternatives.

The result: a clear problem, the need (both family and nursing staff) is clear, emotions are expressed and discussed and cooperating to create a solution.

There are three opportunities to provide feedback in the model of Marshall Rosenberg:

1. Say what you feel, tell what your need is and connect by asking. See example Henri & Mike.

2. Tell in your own words what you think the message is. See example oncology.

3. Say what you think the other feels and what needs are involved. Check whether that is the case. See example Alzheimer patient.

3.4 Learning feedback, Tips & Tops

Tips & tops feedback is applied in learning situations, especially when it's related to the 'how to' of a technical approach or learning of a competence. Just like a teacher does in teaching his student all the tricks of his expertise. He gives rewards, he inquires the way the student thinks or he rejects some ideas or practices. And as everyone will remember from his own years at school it's very nice to hear that you've done well. Of course there are also things you didn't understand or comprehend. Wrong thinking, drawing wrong conclusions as a part of the learning process should be given feedback to discover the way of thinking that led to the wrong conclusion. Knowing the initial way of thinking of the student makes it possible for the teacher to explain more specificly where the mistake has been made. Sometimes teachers should be very clear and reject a chosen strategy or solution, because it's obviously wrong. Of course this should always be accompanied with arguments.

Thus we have described the three stages of learning to deal with feedback.

Step 1   APPOINT WHAT IS GOOD

Even though people make mistakes in communication, there's always something done well. Someone who is learning (for instance giving feedback, giving bad news interviews or trying to influence his children) always does at least something good. And it's nice to hear that. There's a natural tendency to do things in the right way. Nobody wakes up with the thought to do things wrong and to enjoy those failures. In the contrary, people will make an effort to realize their intended actions. When this is recognized and outspoken, the receiver will appreciate that. Besides this pleasant feeling when receiving comments, the feedback serves a purpose. You hear what went well, probably including specific details. For people who are doubting it's really important to hear what is done right. That step transforms the doubt in knowing for sure. His confidence grows and the skill increases.

What I like in your acting is ... ...

At least give positive feedback on his efforts, even when the result is wrong. This recognition will lead to further trying.

Step 2 ASK FOR EXPLANATION

Maybe you saw how the student tries to do his best, very motivated. Nevertheless you have questions like "why is he doing so?" Maybe he has chosen for a different strategy, maybe he's been uncertain somewhere in the process and chooses wrong. It will help you and him if you understand his way of thinking. Then you know exactly what feedback (positive or negative) to give. Maybe you'll discover the student did it all on purpose, he wants to follow his own insights in his own way. Even though you might not agree, it provides clarity.

Can you explain to me why you ... ...

(So I understand your way of thinking)?

Step 3 SAY WHAT YOU WOULD DO DIFFERENT

The final step. You see and hear what the other does. Perhaps he does things wrong and thus gets no results. Perhaps he does things differently, with which he still gets his results. But that could be done much faster or better.

You know you have the best and appropriate way for a good result. This allows you to benefit the other. And the best way to do so, is in a "how I would do that is ...." remark.

I would do that differently, because ... ...

I do that differently, because ... ...

The explanation, the arguments are necessary of course. Because only then you teach the other, then you support him and deliver reasons for reconsideration why he should change his behavior and to move over to your point of view. But, and this is perhaps the most important gain, he also can decide and try a different form himself. People almost always want to decide what to do by themselves. Of course it can occur that someone chooses for a different way. If not already explained in step 2 this is the place where the research should take place.

Application

This method is most suitable for learning new behavior or skills. Many instructors work in this constructive way. With this method you are clear about what you want and why. You also offer that to the student. You connect to his learning process.

Pitfall

There are no real pitfalls in this approach, at least when we focus on the learning process. Applied in the communication process there could be an objection. Right and wrong in communication is a difficult one. So it can easily lead to unpleasant discussions. "You say so! I think differently! You want me to ....! I think it has to be .....! "

This clarifies that conversations where the goal is to understand each other, you better apply the BEIR-model or Marshall Rosenbergs' feedback model with compassion.

TOPS & TIPS FEEDBACK

FROM.............................   TO:............................

1. *WHAT I LIKE IN YOUR ACTING IS:*
   ....
   ....
   ....
   ....
   ....

2. *CAN YOU EXPLAIN WHY YOU DO/CHOOSE FOR*
   ....
   ....
   ....
   ....
   ....

3. *WHAT I WOULD DO DIFFERENT IS:*
   ....
   ....
   ....
   ....
   BECAUSE...
   ....
   ....
   ....
   ....

3.6 Solution-focused feedback

3.6.1 Introduction

Providing feedback has so far focused on what's wrong. Sounds logical, why should feedback otherwise be given? With analyzing and providing feedback we find out what the problem is and what solutions are suitable. Feelings that come in a fix, needs that are made deficit, behavior that doesn't meet the requirements you stated. Then we look for and try to find the best solution. A very logical approach, but problem-oriented. In the search for causes it's like oil on water, very quickly enlarged to a bigger problem.

Typical reactions are shown by the defending responses: "you don't know all", "you should also look at….", "that's not only my responsibility but also …", "I have no influence on all aspects of this problem….." etcetera. In this way people try to escape, do not take their responsibility, even suggest that you exaggerate, to run away.

Solution-focused feedback is much more a real and positive conversation than the other feedback methods. Although the BEIR-method and Marshall Rosenberg's method also (should) lead to a good conversation, now it all starts with a conversation.

3.6.2 Keep it SIMPLE

In the solution-focused feedback the SIMPLE approach is a very useful.

1. Concentrate on Solutions

   The solution-focused feedback prefers not talking about the occurring problem or further analyzing. Of course, you have to agree about an existing problem, but the focus lies on "how do we solve, instead of how is it caused".

2. **I**n-between

There is an explicit appeal to work together to find solutions. What could you do to reduce the wrong behavior or to prevent it? Which behavior has already been there and causes no problems? Can that behavior be used again or more often?

The solution-focused communication method aims at a constructive and positive way of approaching people. Especially at moments when emotions show up (especially guilt, disappointment, confusion) it shows its value.

3. **M**ake use of agreements

Talk about all arguments. See which arguments support each other. Look for the arguments about which you differ so little, that they aren't worth arguing. At last, state which arguments you disagree about. Many times you'll discover that 80-90% of the arguments both of you can agree with. Often the other 10-20% will solve by itself if you're focused on the 80-90%.

4. **P**ossibilities

In this method the feedback and asking to perform differently is highly based on arguments. The focus lies on how different behavior will contribute to your well being. The arguments you use should preferably go in that direction. Focus on possibilities, have a creative and exploring mind.

5. **L**anguage

Use simple language, don't try to impress people with words. In the contrary, try to be as clear and inviting as possible. Use the language that's appropriate for the situation and people involved.

Use simple questions: "how do we treat this?" or "how have we treated that in the past?" are very useful questions.

6. Each case is a different case. Avoid the limiting "ah again or always the same" remark. Each case will turn out to be really different. Another context, with other people involved, with another goal, with another emphasis. Every case should be treated as a different case. And every new case can deliver new opportunities and possibilities.

Of course it's good to learn lessons. What created the problem and what promotes or reduces it? This analyzing may happen afterwards. Try to learn lessons from the past to use them in the future. But: many communication problems really don't need to be analyzed, not even afterwards.

3.6.3 Three basics in the equality of relation

During discussions there are some guidelines to improve the quality of that discussion and the created solution. To take care of equality in relationships it's not only useful, but even a must.

Three principles promote this equality:

1. People can choose

Because everybody's able to think, they're also able to consider advantages and disadvantages (the internal processing of the arguments). Followed by an evaluation, it's possible to make a well-considered and well-defined choice. When both are allowed to take responsibility in this way, the choices that have been made will highly support the acceptance and the consequences that belong to that choice.

WHAT DO I WANT? WHAT DO I WISH? WHAT DO I THINK IS NICE? WHAT WOULD BE A SOLUTION FOR ME?

- *I would like it if you were more approachable.*
- *I like it if you listen to me.*
- *I wish you took more care of ... ...*

You can conceive this step as showing your opinion about something. And everybody is entitled to have his own opinion.

2. People are active

Each person strives for a situation in which he feels good. This probably guides all his actions. He seeks answers and solutions to "problems and difficulties" he encounters on his way. This means that two persons both will and should be active and looking for what supports their well-being. Stating what you want means not only stating a meaning or need. More important are the underlying arguments, because arguments will give a lot more insight into your personality. With arguments you'll show what and why something is important for you and what you try to fulfill. If you want that consideration for yourself, it's quite obvious that you deliver it to the other at the same time. Both of you will try to create the best position in an active way.

BECAUSE: APPOINT THE TROUBLES OR HARRASMENT YOU HAVE DUE TO HIS BEHAVIOR IN ARGUMENTS

- *Because then happens ... ...*
- *Because due to this I cannot ... ...*
- *Because the effect for me is that I ... ...*

Identify arguments with some pertinent points that apply to you. Ask whether the other person wants to talk to you about these arguments or discuss them with you. Ask him what arguments he has for continuing his initial behavior. Don't force somebody else to agree with you. Because just like you, he may have his own opinion and underlying arguments. Ask him about his arguments and try to understand his concerns and criteria.

This step of exchanging arguments (over and over again), can quickly lead to discussion. Especially where the start of a discussion is emotional, the new arguments will probably be accompanied with new emotions. If this reaction occurs a clean and rational communication and feedback should be avoided. Feedback and discussion with compassion is then much more appropriate.

3. People want to be respected

Everybody wants respect for what he experiences or feels in relation to other people. Everybody may have his –own- feelings how strange, stupid, nice or overreacting they are. How another one feels is surely very important but should be your secondary concern. You are the one to take care of first. And: agree to disagree.

Also ask the same questions to him, from his point of view. If necessary: help him.

ASK FOR WHAT YOU WANT, SUGGEST YOUR SOLUTION, DISCUSS AND MAKE AN APPOINTMENT

- *Do you have a suggestion how I can meet your motives?*
- *If we do the following……. we both profit.*
- *What do you think about it? Would you agree? What should be added to make it better?*
- *I suggest……. or what do you think about it, what do you suggest?*

Look for solutions, ask them, deliver them, make an appointment and transform them into action so your problem is solved. This is a much nicer way to cooperate instead of the usual search for the cause and blaming the other. Because the latter approach almost always leads to more problems than before.

Both of you have opinions and arguments. You've asked the other about his arguments and vice versa. It's just a matter of showing respect for each other.

And then there's the moment that you let the other one know that you're satisfied (or not) and perhaps have a solution. The possible reactions are:

- The other one agrees with the solution very quickly.

  Ok, end of the story.

- He may still have a different opinion; then keep on asking. Keep on asking how he would like to solve the problem and especially be curious about his arguments and keep asking about them (respect!). Really listen to him; perhaps his arguments contain information that you haven't considered yet. The more you ask and show that you want to fully understand the other and are even willing to learn from him, the more he'll do for you.

  If you want to be heard, then hear the other!

- It becomes clear that you won't come to an agreement. An entirely new situation arises, in which other skills are more appropriate like negotiation, acceptance and leadership.

- The number of arguments that you continue to disagree with are often not the most important. Continuing with the points of agreement already create change. If these disagreements and differences in assessment remain, both do accept this and agree to disagree.

3.6.4 Appreciative feedback

Appreciative feedback is derived from the appreciative inquiry approach and is a real solution focused approach. Especially useful in contexts where a broad commitment is required. The provided feedback relates to former situations in which desired behavior, skills, insights, strategies, performance already were present. Maybe just once, maybe twice or more often. The appropriate question would be how these former experiences could be repeated, used again and/or applied in contexts where application is a real and expected solution.

The eliciting key questions are

- How could you do this otherwise or better?
- Have you seen or experienced an example of yourself or another person which was better and can we use it?
- How can or do we repeat this behavior?

The underlying assumption is that there are always examples (either from yourself or from others) in which you saw or heard how a desired behavior already occurred or was applied. By asking questions about those examples, you recall them in your memory again and at the same time create new thoughts and ideas. The investigation of the own memory or examples from other people (in other contexts) will always bring an answer. Maybe very small, maybe very differently, maybe very unexpectedly. The appreciative feedback is a very kind and non-forcing way to elicit useful thoughts. This almost always creates motivation to search and to consider.

Simply repeat what works and make that to your own behavior. Sometimes it appears that it not even needs to be discussed. The strategy to recognize a 'working behavior', then adapt to it and followed by repetition makes it a great learning tool. Also a well known strategy, because we see it applied by children in a quite natural way. A kind of modeling the other, followed by 'copy-paste' behavior.

The appreciative inquiry method of communication focuses on the contributive, the positive and the respectful approach of people. Especially in contexts when communication creates a lot of discussion about assumed pro's & con's, it shows its value. Its approach builds on the knowledge that is present in a group or individuals.

The simple question: "where did we treat a problem like this before and how did we do that and how can we repeat that?" creates great openness and ideas.

3.7 Confusing or harmful feedback

Confusing or harmful feedback is for example

- Covered feedback,
- The sandwich feedback
- The metaphor,
- The slap in the face,
- The hang-your-self approach.

In some situations however the application of these methods could still be useful. But there's still the risk to cause so much damage that they should better not be used.

3.7.1 Covered feedback

The feedback message weakened by reducing the severity of the feedback. Weakening is done by showing examples where the feedback receiver acts well besides the wrong behavior. And you also know that there were circumstances why something could go wrong quickly. Submission excuses itself.

This kind of feedback makes the meaning of the feedback less clear for the other. The learning effect is decreasing, because it gives only a vague indication of what kind of change is expected.

"You were too late at that important meeting. And sure, I know you always try to be in time and you have a very business schedule and I also know that at the time there are many traffic jams in the city; so probably you'll be in time the next time."

3.7.2 The sandwich

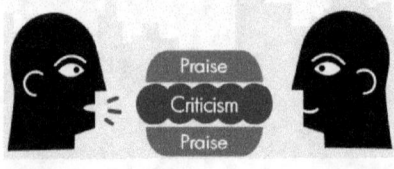

Sandwich Feedback Technique

First something good, then the wrong part, followed by something good again. This creates a smokescreen of vague messages. As if the necessary feedback should not be given. It sounds like the feedback giver fears to express himself in a clear way and to speak freely from the heart.

"Well you know, I really liked it when you said to Jim he should take care of his relationship with customers. That's the kind of feedback someone profits from. To you I would say that you could be even more direct than you are now. But that's a minor part in the whole repertoire you show in all your contacts with people. I think you will develop yourself into a great people manager."

3.7.3 The metaphor

Feedback, only in this shape, makes it very confusing. A comparison with an example situation is made. Many times mythical, a fairytale, a publicly known overrated example is used. The real situation is kept aside, but the conclusion you must draw from the metaphor must be understood as explicit feedback for that real situation.

By using metaphors another charge at the feedback is quickly given. The example (usually heavily enlarged) should deliver a clear idea of the consequences packed in a different way. The listener has the challenge to discover the exact meant feedback hidden in that story. Many times it appears that this feedback isn't recognized at all or is wrongly understood.

The defense is this: "it's really not like you say in your example" or "Now you really exaggerate".

"You know, the effects of coming too late at an appointment is just like that case you may have heard of. The project team of the renovation of that famous museum came together sometimes and made a plan. But because the light expert wasn't involved from the beginning, they missed essential information. The whole plan had to be changed and the project was delayed for many months."

3.7.4 The slap-in-the-face

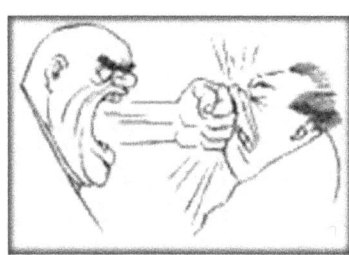

From the experienced problems (why you want to give feedback) state a clear accusation. The feedback giver accuses the other. The use of words like "you did ... ." or "you are ... ..." are often used.

YOU messages with an accusing and pointing finger and emotional tone. The other person only rests the choice between defense or apologize. A real conversation is hardly possible anymore, because the accusation is rude, creates unsafety and feels like being literally attacked. It's likely that a nasty debate is the result instead of a constructive conversation.

"You do that very wrong. You are responsible if this team runs out of time, because you come too late time after time."

3.7.5 The hang-yourself method

Conduct a conversation in such a way that the feedback recipient only can say that he was wrong. It looks as if the rope around the neck is getting tighter bit by bit, piece by piece. All facts are told in a sequence wherein he listens to as well as judges his own behavior. The feedback giver is talking in such a way, evocative, half accusing, interpreting facts unilaterally with one purpose: the feedback receiver can only admit his faults and punish himself. "I'm guilty, I shouldn't have done that! OK, OK! You're right, how can I correct it?" In this approach not the problem and its solution are the main purpose, but the recipient as a person. The hang-yourself way focuses on the person instead of the playing the ball. The recipient soon feels caught, framed, manipulated and is dissatisfied about this approach. The next time he'll be alert and distrust the other. Obviously a personal or working relationship will be damaged by this approach.

You understand that by coming too late, the whole meeting is delayed. Yes. And that has as a result that some scheduled points can't be discussed. Yes. And because of that we can't save on the expenses of the office right in time. Yes. And that means that in our monthly survey we don't succeed in the business policy. Yes. So your being late has tremendous consequences for all of us, How do you think to solve these. Uh....

Some other effects

Covered feedback, the sandwich and the metaphor: preferably don't apply them. "Halfway measures are worse than none". The intention and thus the effect of the feedback are too unclear.

The metaphor can be used as an extra clarification, next to other methods. The slap-in-the-face leads to quarrels → is reproachful → is accusing → leads to defense → and provides counterattack.

Very direct feedback is possible, but only when agreed to do so on the beforehand and there is enough attention to the care for each other afterwards.

The hang-yourself approach is tedious and deteriorates relationships. It has a pretty pedantic nature.

The advantage is that the step-by-step approach delivers a lot of the understanding. You know exactly what's going on. Such an analysis could be made in a better way.

4

AXES OF CHANGE

learning to give and to receive feedback

4.1 Introduction

In the wish to learn giving feedback in organizations, in teams, but also at home perhaps the most asked questions are

"How do I do that?"

"How do I say that ..... without offending someone?"

How do you tell the other that you have reasons to think completely different about a certain topic? Having a different opinion without problems. By telling you don't want to cause a nasty atmosphere and no hassle or angry faces afterwards. How can you give feedback and keep everyone happy?

The feedback methods described in chapter four are clear and can be learned in training. But the results are often unsatisfactory. People understand the theory pretty well and they know exactly what to do. They seem to understand and to apply them temporarily and then return to the old style. Again: saying nothing or suppressing the present annoyance and causing damage to relationships as a result. It's very obvious that just practicing a method is not enough. Is learning to give feedback really so difficult?

And the answer is twofold.

- Yes it's difficult, if you do it in the wrong way.
- No it's not difficult, if you approach it properly.

Any new behavior remains if it delivers advantages and creates worth for you personally. When you want to learn how to give feedback in another way and replace the old style with a new one this only will succeed when the new style offers you more. It appears that just applying a method isn't enough. Being well prepared, evaluate and readjust the style, to create an own style is the challenge too.

 With the 'axes of change-model' of L. Michael Hall it is explained that there is a precise order how to learn a new skill or behavior. The model shows the steps in a learning process. From desire to fulfillment. With regard to motivation, decision making, implementation, evaluations and solidification. Skipping one or more steps repeatedly causes the fall back to the old style.

Another reason for failures could be our optimism. We think that within just a few days the new style could be learned. And that's a false thought. Just like people in sports, the skill of giving and receiving feedback should be practiced time after time, again and again. Until there's a feeling of certainty and confidence and you became a master.

4.2 AXES OF CHANGE[8]

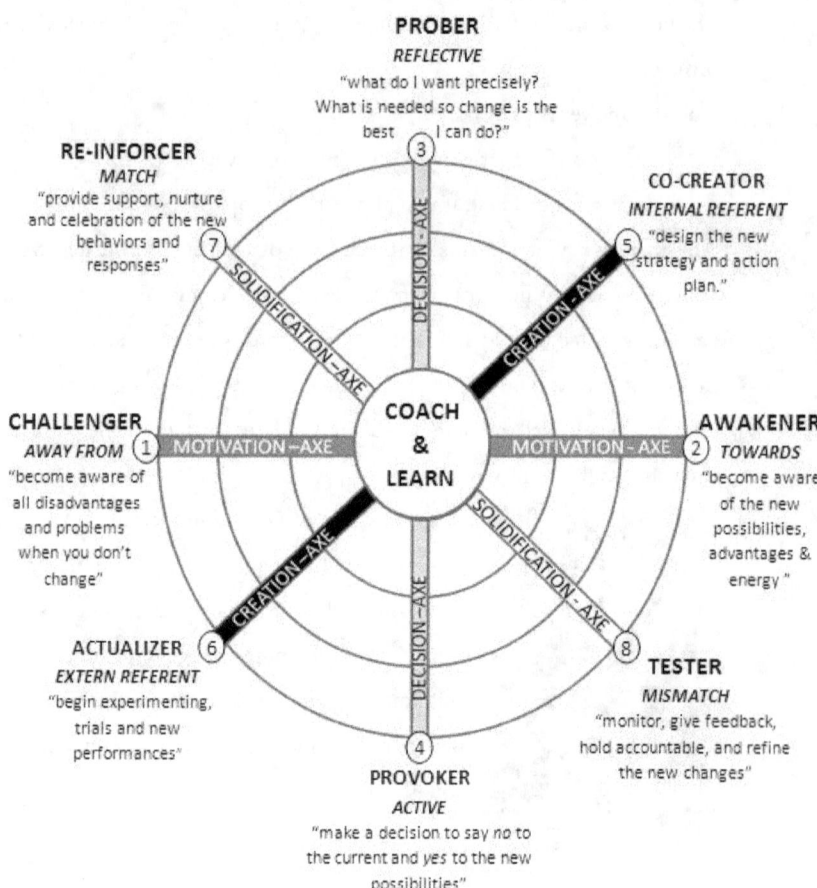

[8] THE AXES OF CHANGE Introducing a New Generative Change Model
Coaching Change: Meta-Coaching Volume 1. Published by Neuro-Semantic Publications.
Written by L. Michael Hall, Ph.D., cognitive psychologist and modeler of excellence in self-actualization, Executive Director of ISNS. www.neurosemantics.com; meta@acsol.net

What is the Axes of Change model?

As a model or template for working with the change process 'The Axes of Change model' uses the key mechanisms or variables that are involved in change.

These include:

- *The Energy-Motivation stage:* creating sufficient emotional energy, motivation, and creative tension to feel both the need and the desire for the change. This gives us propulsion for change: away from the aversions and pains and toward the attractions and pleasures.

- *The Decision stage:* creating sufficient understanding and knowledge about what to change, why it doesn't work, and generating enough decision power to create a readiness for change. This gives us the encouragement to say *no* to the current way of thinking, feeling, and acting and *yes* to the possibilities of a generative change.

- *The Creation stage:* creating a specific action plan that describes the change, giving us a step-by-step plan that we can then begin acting on and experimenting with. This gives us the plan to implement and actualize in real life.

- *The Solidifying stage:* creating specific rewards and support for the new actions that we celebrate a champion. Meanwhile continue the testing and monitoring, and using the received feedback to make our new behavior richer, fuller, and more integrated into our new habit and way of responding. This gives us a way to keep solidifying the change so that it becomes part of who we are and so that it ecologically fits into our life style.

The Axes of Change model describes the process of how to develop new behavior (feedback) following the sequence of eight development steps according to four related axes. In a clear step by step approach it points out how you learn new behavior and skills and how a desired outcome is achieved. The model is originally developed for and used in the meta-coach training by L. Michael Hall as a coach model.

4.3   New behavior and skills

1.   *motivation-axis: WHAT I DON'T WANT ANYMORE!*
     Use the challenger-state, focus on "away from the pain" and become
     aware of all disadvantages and problems if you don't change.

I want to get rid of my fear to speak in public, my incompetence to say what I want, and being afraid to hurt the other one.

An internally focused action:
Write down what you no longer want. What is bothering you? What do you regret afterwards or causes a dissatisfaction because again you gave no feedback. You know you should give feedback, but you're afraid that people think you're not that nice of a person anymore. You're afraid of the reactions that may follow on your feedback. Describe exactly what you don't want to do (behavior & thoughts) any longer.

2.   *motivation-axis: WHAT DO I WANT?*
     Use the awakener-state, focus on "towards what I really want" and become
     aware of the new possibilities, advantages and feel how it energizes."

I give feedback, very brightly, clearly and in an honest way, both in matters of cooperation in the personal attitude and in giving 'learning feedback' (as described in chapter 3.5). I'm able to criticize people even if the feedback is related to more personal feelings and issues.

Also an internal target action.

Knowing exactly what you want is the important second step. Your brains need to have an accurate set of goals and targets. Without a well developed goal you certainly don't achieve the desired results.

For example: I want to give my opinion, in I-language and before I do I ask the other person whether he has the time at that moment to listen to me and ask at the end of the interview if he has tips I can use to improve my feedback.

I accomplish this goal within one week and will make an appointment with my partner so he can coach me.

3. *decision-making axis:* THE DECISION IN THE MIND

Use the prober-state in a self-reflective way and ask yourself:

"What exactly do I want? What is needed so change is the best I can do?"

I decide to actually give feedback in a really different way. I've thought about it and I know what it costs and yields. Either: give feedback or leave it behind. I have judged for myself I'm really able to give feedback and it can really be a skill I want to master and I also think it belongs to me.

It's a targeted internal action.

I know what I want, I also know what benefits I will get as a result. I also know the disadvantages, the costs. Advantages include that I feel much more comfortable with myself and a possible disadvantage could be that my colleagues just label it as a strange and odd behavior in a way they don't know me. In your mind you look for as much arguments as possible in order to be confident and give feedback according to your opinions and arguments.

4.   *decision-making axis:* THE DECISION IS KNOWN

   Use the provoker-state, actively applied and make the decision to say no to the current and yes to the new possibilities.

Challenge yourself, especially in situations in which you normally tend to be weak, or avoid confronting people. Are you then still decisive to change?
I inform the people in my environment (not only the trusted ones) so they know what I'm doing. Not only for exercising and practicing, but also as a kind of guarantee that I don't relapse into my old behavior. Because I know some people will laugh about me when I relapse or stop it will be a motivator to continue as well. Probably you'll see people often just want to help.

It's an externally oriented action.
Because I've set goals many times but haven't accomplished them, I decide to inform my colleagues, so they know what I'm doing. That means I have to be very confident about my opinions and arguments. When I tell these to others there's a chance I may receive some support. And that could make it a lot easier. And of course, if I stop, there will be a loss of face. And I don't like that. People can help me by provoking me in this part of the change process.

5. *creation axis:* I KNOW EXACTLY HOW I WILL PERFORM

Use the co-creator-state, in an internal referenced way and design the new strategy and action plan.

Now everyone knows that I want to improve the way I give feedback, I'll have to show it too. This creation starts with thinking about the way I'll give feedback.

I'll study the feedback methods that could be appropriate for the given situation and consider whether to use it or not. Using a model step by step makes it much easier to remember. I question myself what other resources I could use.

It's a mainly internal action.

The first times I look for easy examples to give feedback. In my mind I check what approach would be most suitable for the situation. I think about the moment I give feedback, how I can monitor and influence my own tension and state. I think about the words I will use. I may write them down according to the steps of the chosen method. I change perspective as if I am the other person and prepare myself to expected replies. I spend some time to my pitfalls, so I won't slip into that state in a naïve way. I prepare myself to the expected stress and how I can manage my body to become more relaxed and I know belly breathing is an answer to that. I again read the most annoying mistakes I want to avoid in such a conversation.

6. *creation axis:* IMPLEMENTATION

Use the actualizer-state, check your actions in an external referenced way. Begin experimenting, use trials and new performances.

The implementation with which the environment also sees, hears and feels what new behavior I use. The first couple of times when testing the new strategies are recommended to be done in a group of people you trust so you can learn from their feedback. These test cases will be continuously improved while using and applying the received feedback.

A mainly externally oriented action accompanied by internal thought processing.
All preparations are now translated into action. I start giving feedback to someone who is not too resistant and who will probably appreciate my feedback. I ask him in advance whether he has some time for me to talk about a specific subject. I ask him afterwards (and maybe also before) if he wants to give me some advice about how I can improve my feedback.
If this step goes well I give feedback to people who behave increasingly difficult to feedback and reply with a critical respond.

7.   *solidification-axis:* **CELEBRATE THE FIRST**
     SUCCESSES *Use the re-inforcer-state, with a matching (what was done well?) attitude. Provide support, nurture and celebrate the new behaviors and responses.*

In my workbook I describe exactly how I actually performed. I evaluate what could be done better, what went well and what I have to pay more attention to the next time. I'm not firmly critical to my actions. I focus on what went well, even for a step that actually didn't work out well. I especially rethink whether my preparations were OK, or what could be prepared better to create bigger success. This evaluation will give me more and more self-confidence about the fact that this way of giving feedback is the right approach for me. For now and in the future.

Party-time: recognize the things that went well and celebrate your first victories. Experience that the new style is really possible and delivers a good feeling and that should be celebrated.

It's an internally and externally oriented action.

Oh it's the first time I said something! I gave feedback and it feels great! I always wanted to do that and that fact in itself is a reason to celebrate. I note my evaluations in my workbook, so I know why I should celebrate and where I can improve or could maintain my new behavior. Because I also strive to improvements (certainly in the beginning of my learning process) I keep track of all these facts in a workbook. For future use or to recall great experiences at a weak moment.

8. *solidification-axis:* IMPROVEMENTS TO ADD

> *Use the tester-state in a really mismatching attitude.*
> *Monitor, give feedback, hold accountable, and refine the new changes"*

In the two former steps you also received information where the new behavior still was unsatisfying. You have to adjust and improve. Step by step until perfection is achieved. Of course you keep on practicing giving feedback. Maybe you have to go back to step 3 where the internal decision (Was it right? Was it stated in the right way? Did you involve all consequences of your decision? Etc.) was made. Or go back to step 6 where you implemented your new strategy. Did you choose the right words, the right moment, the right state or could you change things in a way that the outcome is even more appropriate?

Internal process

Internally decide what step needs to be changed or improved. Describe what you've improved compared to the original plan. Maybe there's some old (un)expected pitfall behavior, or a typical characteristic habit in your communication style, or personal property. Decide what you're going to do about this. Be critical without judging, look for clues and hints to improve. Maybe you can refine the new behavior to become really suitable for you. Create your own style in applying the feedback. Maybe with more humor, maybe more friendly, maybe with more compassion, maybe more directly. Be honest to yourself, without self-rejection. Give yourself the opportunity (time & mistakes) to learn.

4.4 The master process

'Practice is mother of all learning'.

Learning something new, many people start really innocent, not knowing what they actually do wrong or incomplete. You start unconsciously incompetent (UI). You don't know

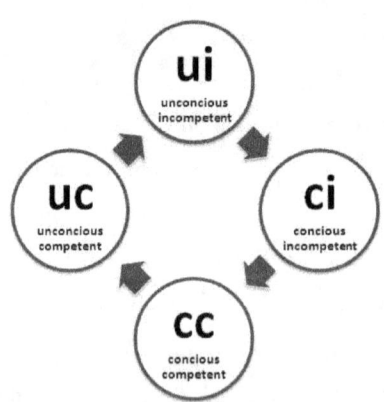

what you don't know. Discovering the blind-spot in your behavior is the first step to take. Attention and self-exploration makes you aware about the topics to work on. The next step is consciously practicing with new learned behavior. Again and again to achieve improvements, to grow from novice to more experienced. This happens mainly in the second phase in which you're consciously incompetent (CI). The more you practice, the more skilled you become. Suddenly you experience that you're fully in control of the new behavior. Maybe there's still a conscious following the method-steps as a guideline, but you know them completely (CC). In this phase the competence is really enhanced, due to all the practicing and exercising. You're consciously competent. And then suddenly there's the moment when you no longer have to think about steps, words, attitudes, and so on. The behavior is fully integrated. It's a part of your skills and expertise. You can easily and effortlessly apply the new behavior in very different situations. You are unconsciously competent (UC).

Suddenly you notice (or somebody pointed to a new blind spot in your behavior) that there's still something new to learn or to be improved and the cycle starts again.

The crux of successful learning is obviously "practicing, exercising & experiencing". Essential to this learning process is receiving feedback. Feedback can make you the champion in applying the wanted behavior. Just compare it with athletes. Olympic medals can only be won by training, over and over again and guided by their coaches. And the coaches' job is "to take care for repeated and disciplined trainings and to give suitable and competent feedback to improve the talent". In that way "feedback becomes food for champions".

4.5 The DO'S

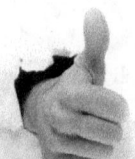

Applying feedback will be a lot easier when you use the following tips:

- Ask before you give feedback, whether it's OK to talk about something right here and now. If you ask it in an open way and the other says yes, there's already a basic willingness to receive feedback. This is the opposite of the attacking way and which leads to a defending response. When somebody answers with "not now", ask when it's an appropriate moment to talk.

- Start learning to give feedback by giving positive feedback. Follow the feedback steps in showing appreciation.

- Ask the other whether he wants to give you feedback. Invite him to do so. Probably he will do so and in a more cooperative way.

- Find people with whom you can spar, people who also learn to give feedback and share experiences.

- Reread the feedback methods and the way to learn these methods with the axes of change regularly.

- Prepare yourself first on paper, write your preparation in a workbook. The value of this is great because you not only read (visual), but you also describe (supported by an internal dialogue) the steps. This method provides a much better storage in your memory, because you use three senses: seeing, hearing and feeling.

- Prepare yourself in your mind, repeat all steps, step by step and visualize them as if you have already applied them.

- Start simple. For the first couple of times it is better to use examples with less emotion and then build up to increasingly difficult situations. Celebrate your successes.

- Note where you encounter your repeating troubles. If these always occur at the same moment, in the same situation, with the same (kind of) persons, with the same feelings then the first priority is to examine what the cause is. Therefore first address your weaknesses and strengthen your skills.

4.6 The DONT'S

What you should avoid doing:

- Listening to skeptics. Listening to people who tease and react with cynicism or counterarguments. They try to make you doubt about your abilities and your work. Sometimes open, but mostly in a hidden way.

- Checking your development with pessimists. The pessimists always find something negative and suck energy. Find the people who really support you!

- Be aware of perfectionists. They always find something that isn't OK or should have done better. Maybe they're right but they also undermine your new energy. In their drive to perfectionism they elicit thoughts like: "I'll never learn to give feedback in an appropriate way" or "I'd better stop!"

  Isolate and honor "the points to be improved", try to incorporate them in your new feedback style. Nothing more and nothing less.

- Don't want to do too much in the beginning. Start with small things. First supply feedback in situations that are easy. The most difficult cases or difficult people can disappoint you very deeply. These disappointments easily create a state in which you want to stop, you disencourage yourself and probably stop the learning process.

But, yes you can! Just like the sports of high jumping you also start with the bar at 30 inches and then after successes you can increase the height. Nobody will start jumping at a height of 60 inches.

- When you start doubting about your abilities and it looks like you will fall back into old behavior, then quickly find someone who may coach you through this part of the process. Avoid the negative ones! You better read and re-read your workbook again and again and enjoy your past successes to get some new energy and enthusiasm.

4.7 Workbook

Keep track of your developments in a workbook!

The learning process will take place in different ways.

For some people it is just enough to read the text and they may already know the techniques and can apply them immediately. Perfect for you if you're one of them.

But others need a lot more direction and support. The best way to start the whole process is with a partner, a buddy, a friend. Make some appointments and agreements how you two want to be "treated & coached". Discuss what support at the different stages would be suitable for each other. Support each other and provide feedback on the learning process. This "peer coaching" will turn out to be a very effective form of learning.

One of the best learning tools is to write down what you intended or tried to do, followed by what you actually did and experienced. This shows exactly in what step of the 'axes of change' you should improve your preparation or performance. Perhaps you discover specific reasons or background information about why things go wrong every time you try.

The second advantage of writing is that the storage in your memory is accessed in several ways. Seeing (the pen writes text), hearing the inner voice and feeling how a pen creates your words and sentences on paper combine three of your senses to learn. Your memory is informed in three ways, so information is recorded much better than in case of just reading.

And finally by recognition you can address your own pitfalls in a better way. What are these pitfalls, when do they occur? What are your successes and when do they occur? And what are the points you still have to work on, or those learning points you temporarily set on hold?

The workbook makes your process quite visible and conscious to you. The workbook together with this book thus contain all feedback notes, alternative texts to use, described examples. The workbook is available at the website www.coachforchange.nl.

EPILOGUE

Providing feedback is a skill. And as any skill, it can be learned.

It's not easy but as this book shows it's certainly achievable. It's not easy because of all the belonging emotions that accompany feedback. Someone who receives feedback will notice that something is said about him. It triggers an internal emotion he's not quite comfortable with and if possible he will avoid this feeling. This leads to discomfort, a kind of a feeling of rejection up to resistance. And indeed, that's not such a pleasant state of being.

As long as the feedback receiver doesn't come into action to this discomfort, it will continue to happen to him. And probably it doesn't matter in what way you give the feedback.

Every improvement of conversation is due to the progress you've made in giving feedback in a respectful way. If that conversation happens and a real dialogue between you two takes place, you will (and also the other) suddenly experience that there's a more open and friendly way to really talk with each other. Even about the difficult things. The willingness to make arrangements will grow, so there's profit for both. No winner or loser, just both will benefit.

Feeling the respect for each other and knowing that you build something great in the relationship is a pleasant, constructive and stimulating thought.

So it makes feedback a wonderful skill what should be and can be used everywhere where people live and work together.

BIBLIOGRAPHY

Books in alphabetical order

- Ronald van Domburg, the appreciative eye
  Atelier Creation, ISBN 9 789460 000010

- Thomas Gordon, P.E.T. in action,
  problems, insights and solutions in parent effectiveness training
  Wyden Books, ISBN 90 289 0458 1

- Berthold Gunster, Yes-but what if it all works?
  Bruna, ISBN 90 229 9144 X

- L. Michael Hall, meta-coaching volume 1
  Neuro-Semantic Publications ISBN 978-1890001261

- L. Michael Hall, MovieMind, directing the Theater of Your Mind
  Neuro-Semantic Publications ISBN 90 202 6054 5

- Paul Jackson & Mark McKergow Solution Focus Theme,
  ISBN 90-5871-043-2

- Lucie Leu, workbook nonviolent communication
  Lemniscaat, ISBN 90-5637-855-4

- Gary B. Lundberg & Joy Saunders Lundberg
  I don't have to make everything all better
  Riverpark Publishing ISBN 978-0140286434

- Nisandeh Neta, elements of success
  Andromeda publishers, ISBN 978-9055001880

- Marshall Rosenberg, nonviolent communication
  Lemniscaat, ISBN 90-5637-854-6

Articles

- Authenta model of nonviolent communication www.authenta.nl
- Michael Hall & Michelle Duval

  the axes of change, part I & II, introducing a new generative change model, www.meta-coaching.org

Coaching to Unleash Human Potential

Neuro-Semantics, and NLP before it, emerged within the heritage of the *Human Potential Movement*. The key leaders in that movement, which during the 1960s to the 1980s revolutionized the fields of therapy, psychology, self-development, leadership and management, business, developmental psychology, etc., were Abraham Maslow and Carl Rogers. They were followed by Fritz Perls, Virginia Satir, and Gregory Bateson. These three people were part of Esalen—the central growth center of the Human Potential Movement. And they were also the first individuals modeled by Bandler and Grinder to create the NLP version of self-actualization.

Until recently this has been unknown and unacknowledged. Yet the very presuppositions of NLP about human psychology and functioning came from the basic premises of the Human Potential Movement. All of this becomes important as NLP and Neuro-Semantics is applied to the emerging field of Coaching. That's because Coaching is uniquely founded upon Self-Actualization Psychology.

In the field of Coaching, there is coaching and then there is *meta*-coaching. *Meta-Coaching* differs by going beyond Performance Coaching to the heights of Developmental Coaching and Transformational Coaching. It "goes meta" to work at a higher level to a client's performance, states, attitudes, and beliefs.

Discover this difference in the *Meta-Coaching trainings* as you explore coaching modalities for unleashing personal power and mastery. The design in coaching is to empower people in developing their best thinking, feeling, speaking, behaving, and relating. It is to tap into hidden and undeveloped potentials, and awakening them. In this, coaching is the premier process for self-actualization.

Consequently, to fully document *the Meta-Coach System* as a leading Coach Training process, Dr. L. Michael Hall, Ph.D. took on the goal in 2002 to write a series of books. The objective was to detail all of the models and processes of "Coaching" using NLP and Neuro-Semantics. The following books provide that documentation at this date (mid-2010).

Meta-Coaching Series

I:	Coaching Change
II:	Coaching Conversations
III:	Unleashed: A Guide to Your Ultimate Self-Actualization
IV:	Self-Actualization Psychology
V:	Achieving Peak Performance
VI:	Unleashing Leadership: Self-Actualizing Leaders and Companies
VII:	The Crucible (due in 2010)
VIII:	Benchmarking (due in 2011)

Complementary books about NLP and Neuro-Semantics

For personality profiling using meta-programs : *Figuring Out People* (2005).

For self-reflexive consciousness and higher levels : *Meta-States* (2005), *Secrets of Personal Mastery* (1999), *Winning the Inner Game* (2007).

For systems thinking : *The Matrix Model* (2003).

For NLP communication model : *User's Manual for the Brain* (1997, 1999), *Movie-Mind* (2002).

For these books & trainings, see
www.neurosemantics.com;
www.self-actualizing.org;
www.meta-coaching.org;
Crown House Publications and Neuro-Semantic Publications;
usa@meta-coaching.org

CoachforChange

Frans Knoben is director, founder & trainer/coach of CoachforChange. After 25 years of experience in healthcare, working in senior & management positions, he has chosen to be a professional trainer & coach. He combines the operational experiences of his lifetime career with managerial insights as trainer/coach.

"How can what is already present in knowledge,
be visualized in skills? "

In particular, his results-oriented approach and coach sessions successfully contribute to the work performance and pleasure of many managers and employees in government, healthcare, education, commercial services and ICT.

The trainings and coaching of CoachforChange show a mix of

o   evoking enthusiasm

o   self-discovery

o   the opposite as a contribution

o   confrontation and humor

o   reflection on the personal context

o   instruction, exercises and learning on the job

o   brain centered learning

o   solidification arrangements

o   energy and self-responsibility

And that's exactly what knowledge transforms to skills.

Training and coaching always start with customization. No general standards. The uniqueness of the individual or organization is treated with respect. Therefore programs are always compiled in co-creative consultation. The conditions under which the training within an organization will be made to a success is a co-creation between committed coaches, trainers and organization.

The trainings of CoachforChange are especially focused on team processes and support them towards desired change and wanted results.

Information & Contact:

Frans Knoben

+31 6 22 52 19 59
info@coachforchange.nl
www.coachforchange.nl

www.ingramcontent.com/pod-product-compliance
Lightning Source LLC
Chambersburg PA
CBHW060635290526
45793CB00001B/262